Sight Reading
CELLO
A progressive method
Grades 6-8

Celia Cobb & Naomi Yandell

Published by
Trinity College London Press Ltd
trinitycollege.com

Registered in England
Company no. 09726123

Copyright © 2020 Trinity College London Press Ltd
Pages 22-25, 46-50, 72-76 © 2004 Trinity College London Press Ltd and © 2004 Faber Music Ltd
Second impression, April 2023

Unauthorised photocopying is illegal
No part of this publication may be copied or reproduced in any
form or by any means without the prior permission of the publisher.

Cover design by RF Design, rfportfolio.com
Printed in England by Halstan & Co, Ltd, Amersham, Bucks.

Grade 6

Lesson 1

- Practise reading ♪. ♬ ♬ ♪. and ♪ ⁊ ♪ in simple time

A **dotted quaver** lasts for ¾ crotchet beat, or three semiquavers.

♪. ♬   ♬ ♪.   and   ♪ ⁊ ♪   each fit into one crotchet beat.

Check the key signature. Look at the time signature, note values and other details, such as extensions and shifts. Then play the whole exercise.

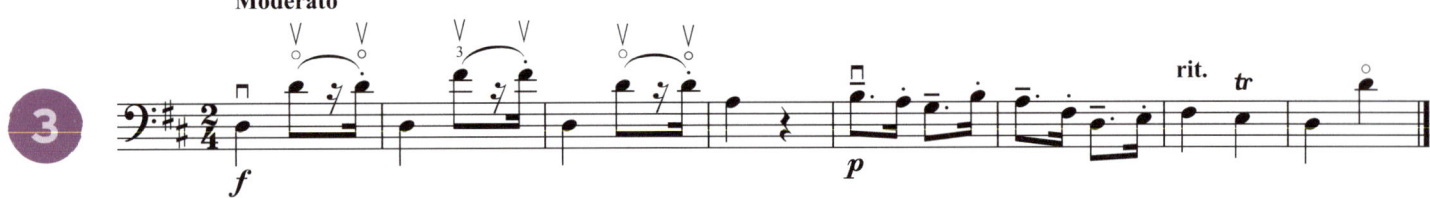

Grade 6

Speed read your part before you play. Check the following:

- Key signature ☐
- Time signature ☐
- Dotted rhythms ☐
- Arpeggio patterns ☐
- Accidentals ☐

- Slurs ☐
- Accents ☐
- Up bow start and retakes ☐
- Dynamics ☐

(This section applies to the duet below.)

 **Duet** Set the pulse. Look at the tempo marking and the time signature, and subdivide the beat to work out a good tempo. Then silently count a full bar before you lead in.

Adapted from Schubert: *Octet* D.803(i)

Always speed read before you sight read so that you are prepared for what is coming up.

3

Grade 6

Lesson 2

- Practise reading ♩. ♫ and ♩. ♬ in compound time

♩. ♫ and ♩. ♬ each fit into one dotted crotchet beat.

Check the key signature. Look at the time signature, note values and other details, such as extensions and shifts. Then play the whole exercise.

Grade 6

Speed read your part before you play. Check the following:

Key signature ☐   Slurs ☐

Time signature ☐   Staccato markings ☐

 rhythms ☐   Dynamics, especially the sudden change in bar 7. ☐

Arpeggio patterns ☐

Duet — Set the pulse. Look at the tempo marking and the time signature, and subdivide the beat to work out a good tempo. Then silently count a full bar before you lead in.

Adapted from Mozart: *String Quartet* K.421 (ii)

Subdividing the dotted crotchet beats will help to ensure that your rhythms are accurate.

Eg in this duet:

5

Grade 6

Lesson 3

- Practise reading in the time signature $\frac{3}{8}$

  three quavers beats in a bar:

Check the key signature. Look at the time signature, note values and other details, such as extensions and shifts. Then play the whole exercise.

1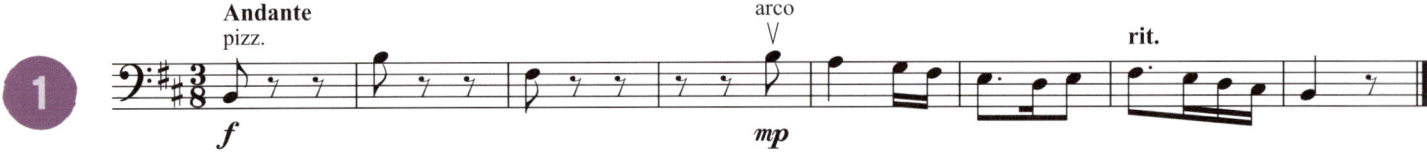

2

3

4

Grade 6

Speed read your part before you play. Check the following:

Key signature ☐   Accidentals ☐

Time signature ☐   Trill ☐

Places where the rhythm and bowing patterns change. ☐   Staccato markings ☐

Set the pulse. Look at the tempo marking and the time signature, and subdivide the beat to work out a good tempo. Then silently count a full bar before you lead in.

Adapted from Mozart: *Symphony* K.318 (ii)

$\frac{3}{8}$ is officially a simple time signature, because each ♪ beat divides easily into two. However, the rhythm-patterns are written in a similar way to those used in the compound time signature $\frac{6}{8}$

Grade 6

Lesson 4

- **Practise reading double stops**

You will sometimes need to play more than one note at the same time:

When you double stop two notes, make sure that you can hear them both – if you can't, tilt your bow towards the missing one to make it sound.

When you play three notes, start with the bottom note and the middle note, then tilt your bow to add the top note as you continue to play the middle note.

Check the key signature. Look at the time signature, note values and other details, such as extensions, shifts and double stops. Then play the whole exercise.

Grade 6

Speed read your part before you play. Check the following:

Key signature ☐   Arpeggio patterns ☐

Time signature ☐   Double up bows and retakes ☐

Double stops ☐   Change of dynamic in bar 5 ☐

Chromatic finger patterns ☐

 Duet   Set the pulse. Look at the tempo marking and the time signature, and subdivide the beat to work out a good tempo. Then silently count a full bar before you lead in.

Adapted from Mozart: *String Quartet* K.525 (i)

At Grade 6, double stops always include one open string.

Grade 6

Lesson 5

- **Practise reading in the key of E major**

This is E major scale. When you play in E major, you will often need to extend or shift.

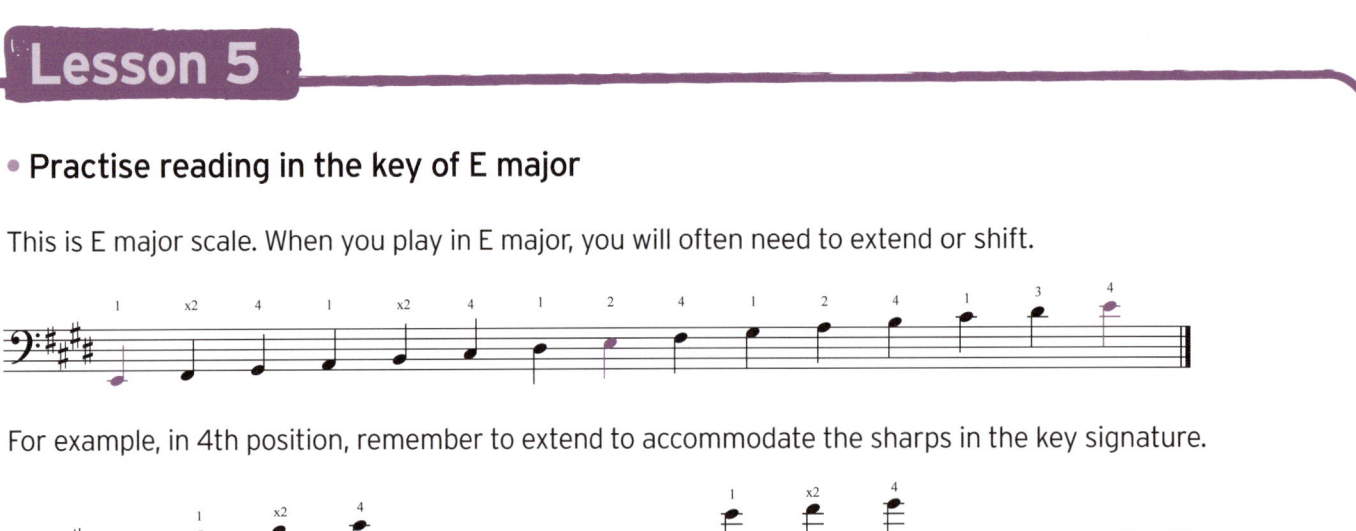

For example, in 4th position, remember to extend to accommodate the sharps in the key signature.

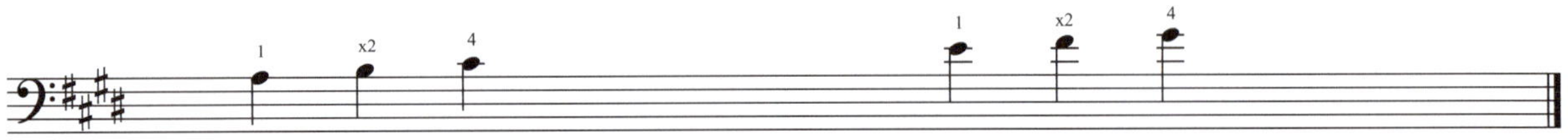

(D string)   (A string)

Check the key signature. Look at the time signature, note values and other details, such as extensions and shifts. Then play the whole exercise.

1 Moderato

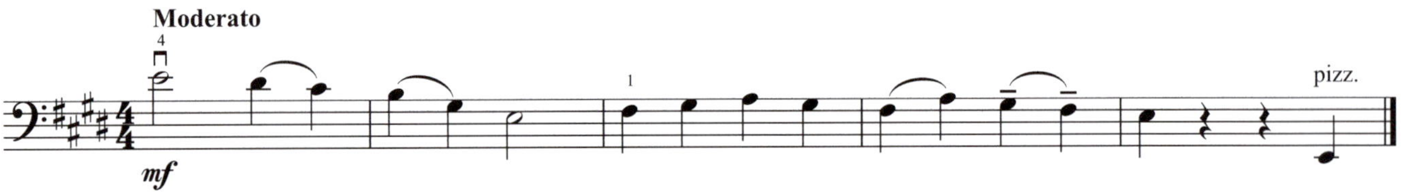

2 Andante

3 Allegretto

4 Andante

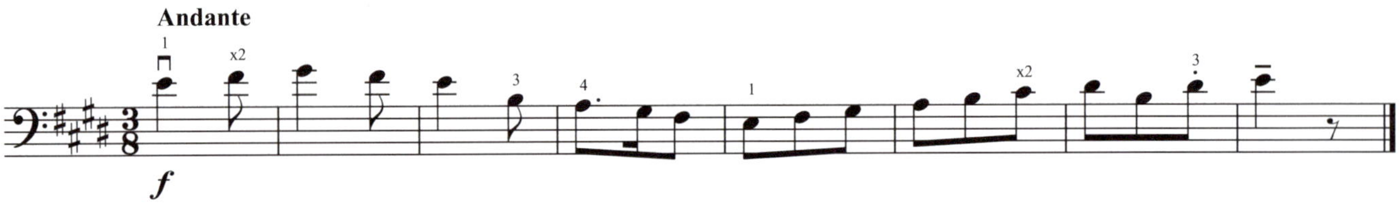

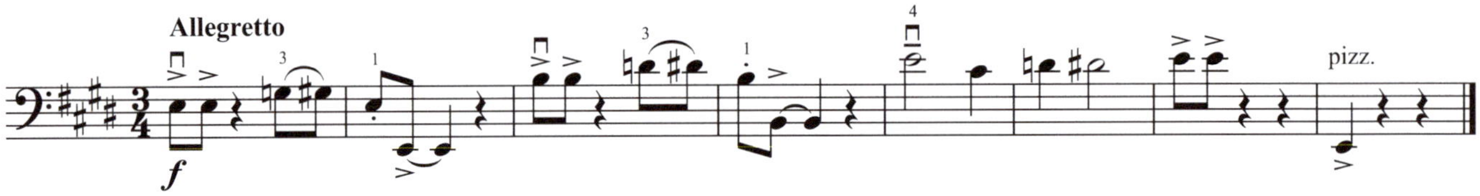

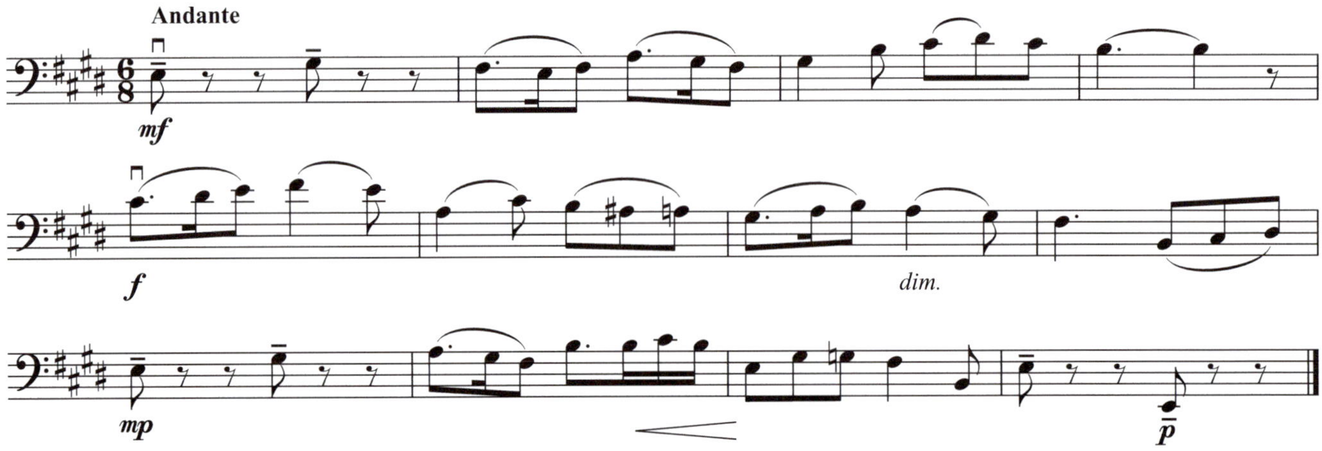

Grade 6

Speed read your part before you play. Check the following:

Key signature ☐   Slurs ☐

Time signature ☐   Retakes and double up bows ☐

Rhythm-pattern change (bar 8) ☐

 Duet Your teacher will need to set the pulse for this duet. Listen carefully to your teacher's part so that you play at the correct tempo.

Adapted from J.S. Bach: *Concerto in E* BWV 1042 (iii)

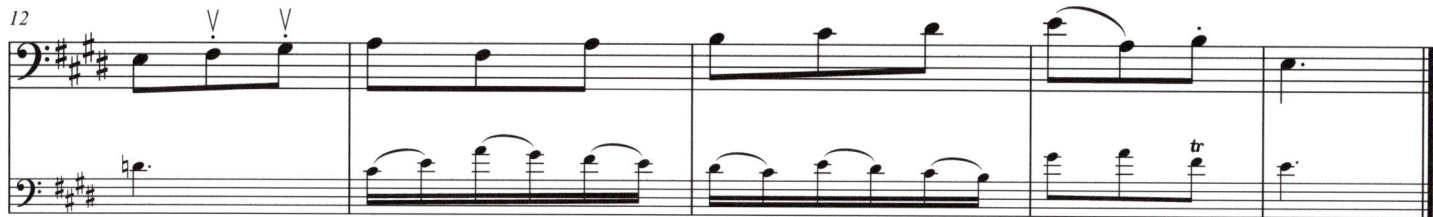

In E major, the sharps in the key signature mean that the only open string you are allowed to play is the A string, unless there is a natural sign to cancel C♯, G♯ or D♯.

Lesson 6

- **Practise reading shifts to lower 2nd position on all strings**

You may sometimes need to shift into lower 2nd position.

A string notes:

D string notes:

G string notes:

C string notes:

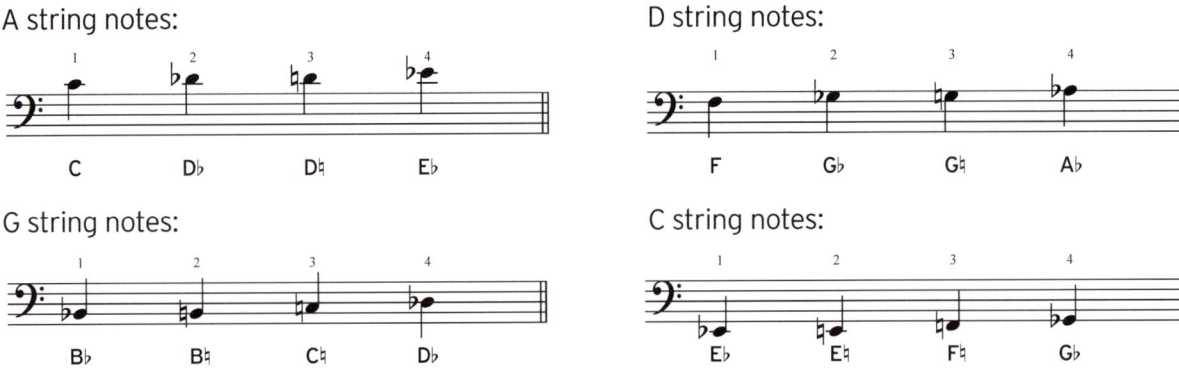

Check the key signature. Look at the time signature, note values and other details, such as extensions and shifts. Then play the whole exercise.

1

2

3

4

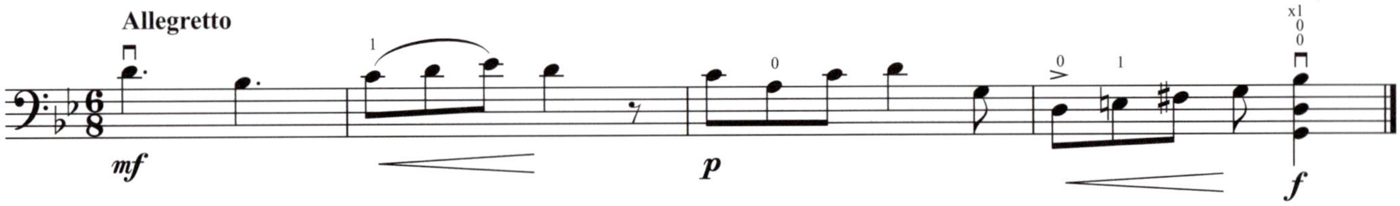

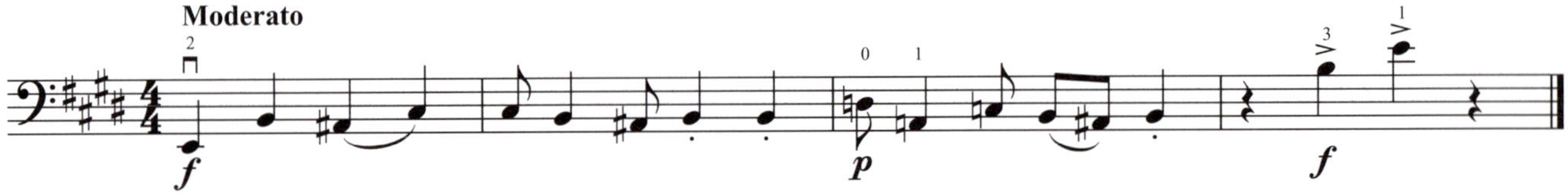

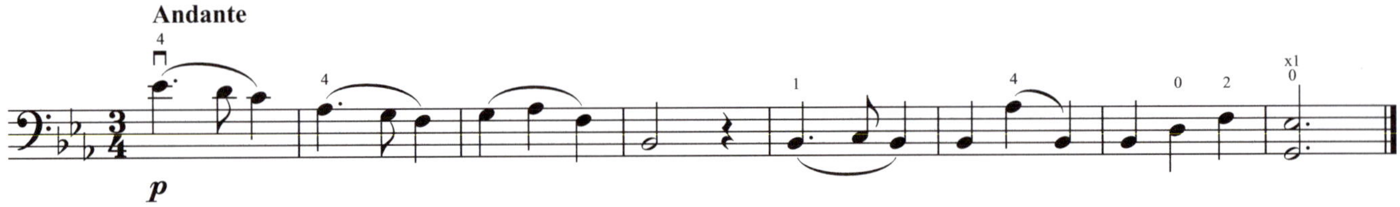

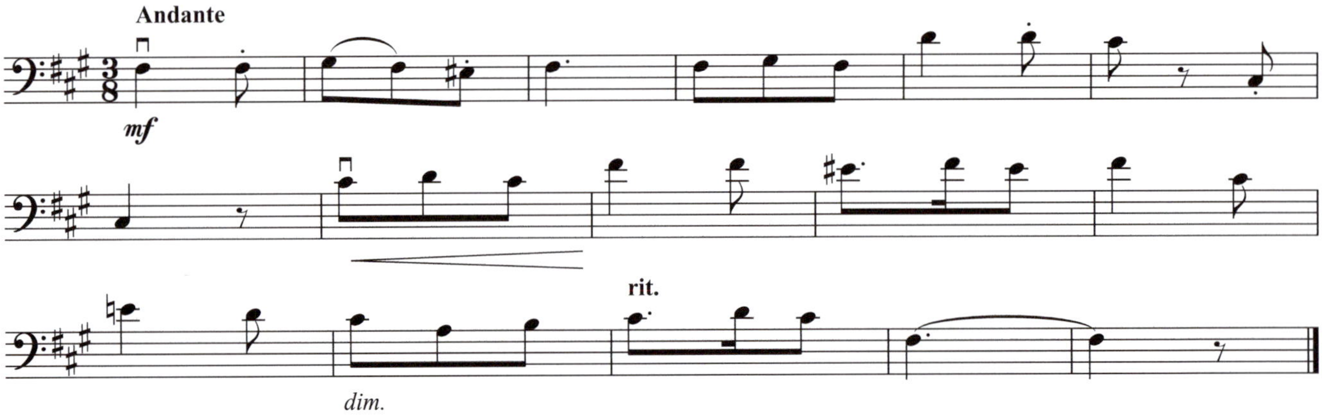

Grade 6

Speed read your part before you play. Check the following:

Key signature ☐   Slurs ☐   ☐

Time signature ☐   Dynamics ☐   ☐

Tied notes and dotted rhythms ☐   Staccato and accent markings ☐   ☐

A flats (high and low) ☐

 **Duet**    Set the pulse. Look at the tempo marking and the time signature, and subdivide the beat to work out a good tempo. Then silently count a full bar before you lead in.

Adapted from Haydn: *String Quartet* Op. 77 No. 1 (ii)

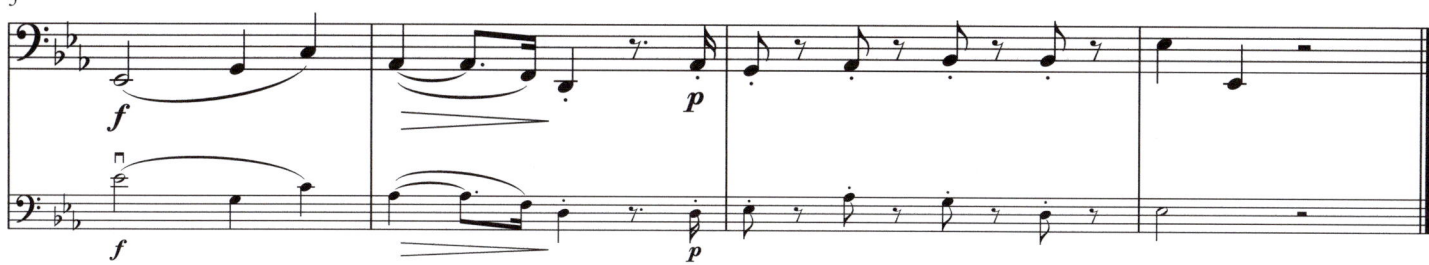

 Subdividing the beat will really help you to play rhythms accurately.

Grade 6

Lesson 7

- **Practise reading in C minor**

E♭ major and C minor share the same key signature.

Keep a look out for accidentals and remember that you will often need to use lower 2nd position and extensions in 4th position because of the key signature.

Check the key signature. Look at the time signature, note values and other details, such as extensions and shifts. Then play the whole exercise.

14

Grade 6

Speed read your part before you play. Check the following:

Key signature ☐ Shifts ☐

Time signature ☐ Accidentals ☐

The change of rhythm-pattern ☐

 Set the pulse. Look at the tempo marking and the time signature, and subdivide the beat to work out a good tempo. Then silently count a full bar before you lead in.

Adapted from Beethoven: *Coriolan* Op. 62

 There is often a choice of fingering. When sight reading you will sometimes have to make snap decisions - this is so much easier if you have quickly looked through the music before you play. It usually makes sense to try to shift as little as possible, especially if the music is fast.

Grade 6

Lesson 8

- Practise reading in the key of A♭ major
- Practise playing in 5th position

A♭ major scale:

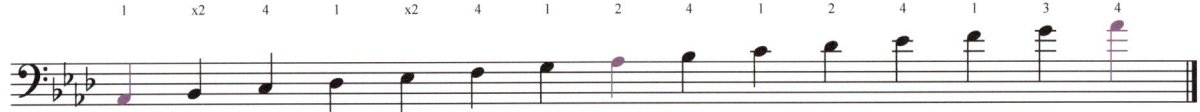

Remember that you will often need to use extensions and shifts because of the key signature.

Check the key signature. Look at the time signature, note values and other details, such as extensions and shifts. Then play the whole exercise.

1

2

3

4

Grade 6

Speed read your part before you play. Check the following:

Key signature ☐ Accidentals ☐

Time signature ☐ Dynamics ☐

Shifts and extensions ☐ Tempo change ☐

 **Duet**   Set the pulse. Look at the tempo marking and the time signature, and subdivide the beat to work out a good tempo. Then silently count a full bar before you lead in.

Adapted from Beethoven: *Sonata No. 8* Op.13 (ii)

In A♭ major, the flats in the key signature mean that the only open strings you are allowed to play are the G and C strings, unless there is a natural sign to cancel A♭ or D♭.

Lesson 9

- **Practise reading shifts to 3rd position on all strings**

You may sometimes need to shift into 3rd position.

A string notes:

D string notes:

G string notes:

C string notes:

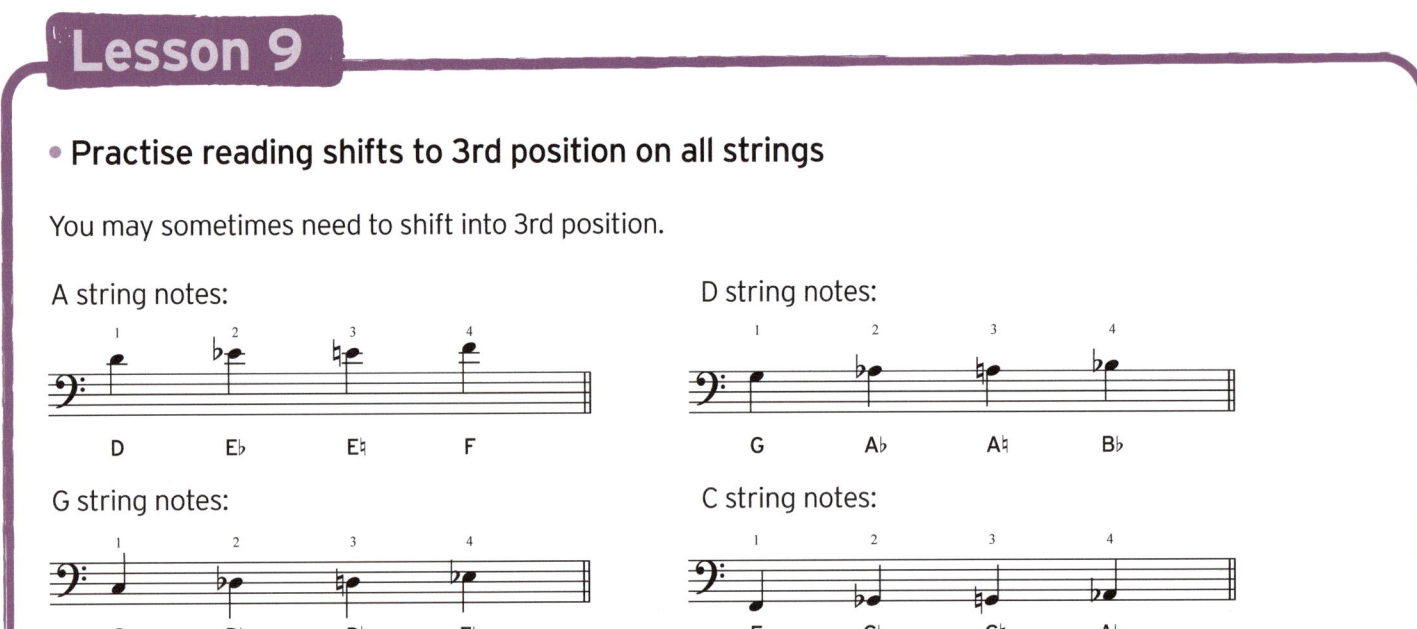

Check the key signature. Look at the time signature, note values and other details, such as extensions and shifts. Then play the whole exercise.

1

2

3

4

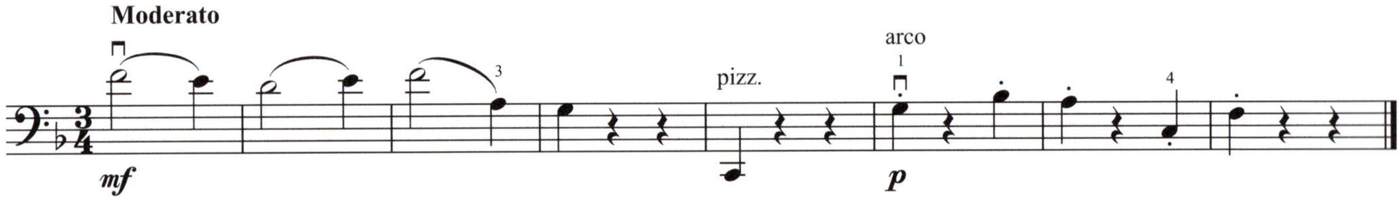

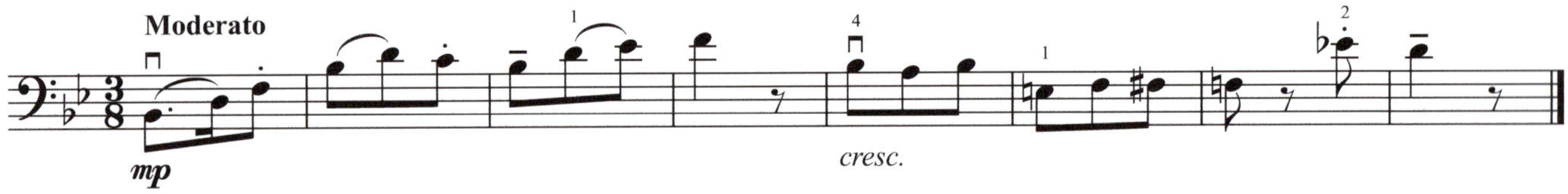

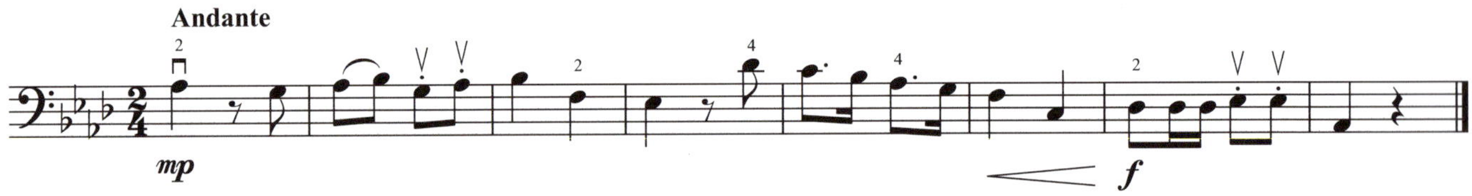

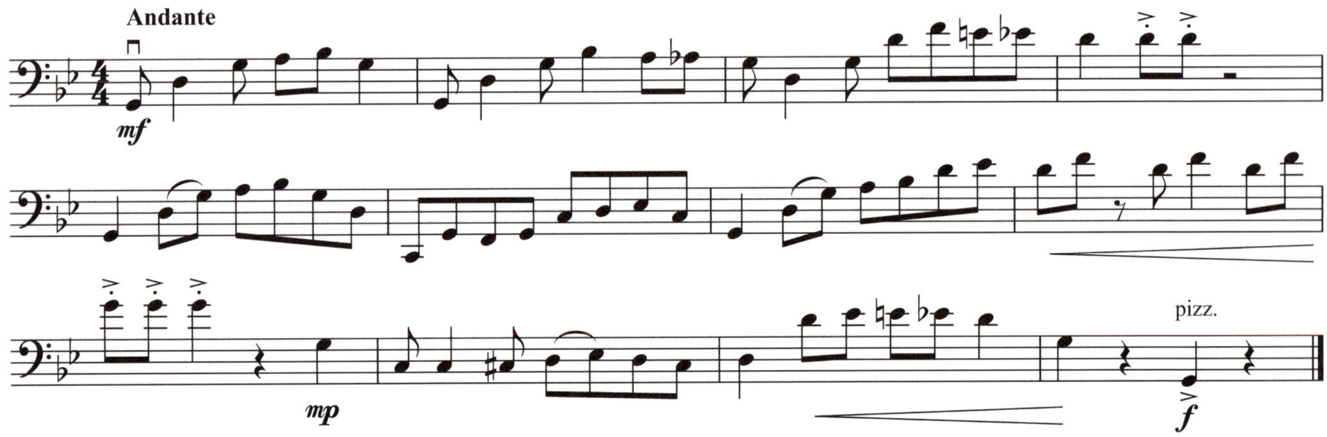

Grade 6

Speed read your part before you play. Check the following:

Key signature ☐   The best position to start in ☐

Time signature ☐   Shifts ☐

The change of rhythm-pattern ☐

 **Duet** Set the pulse. Look at the tempo marking and the time signature, and subdivide the beat to work out a good tempo. Then silently count a full bar before you lead in.

Adapted from Beethoven: *Septet* Op.20 (vi)

It is useful to know the enharmonic equivalent of notes in each position.

Grade 6

Lesson 10

- Revise the meaning of *accelerando* and *a tempo*

Accelerando (or *accel.*) means 'getting gradually faster'.

A tempo means 'in time'. It is an instruction to play at the original tempo after an *accel.*, *rit.* or *rall.*

Check the key signature. Look at the time signature, note values and other details, such as extensions and shifts. Then play the whole exercise.

1.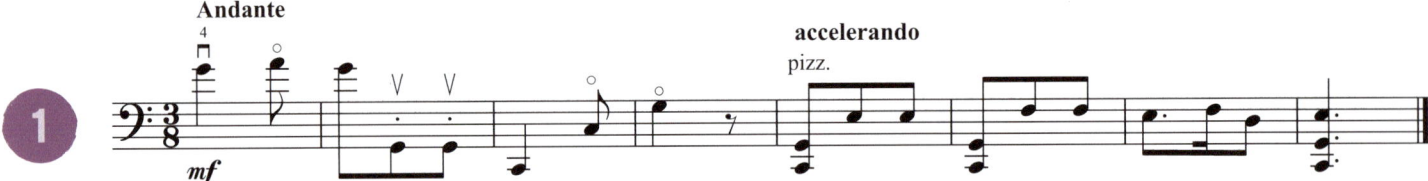

2.

3.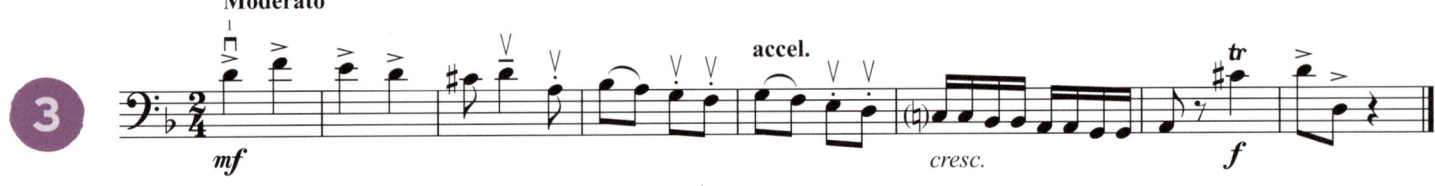

4.

20

Grade 6

Speed read your part before you play. Check the following:

Key signature ☐   Tempo changes ☐

Time signature ☐   Large intervals ☐

Two types of dotted rhythm ☐

Duet — Set the pulse. Look at the tempo marking and the time signature, and subdivide the beat to work out a good tempo. Then silently count a full bar before you lead in.

Adapted from Mahler: *Symphony No.4* (i)

Think carefully about dotted rhythms – remember that ♩. ♪ fits into one crotchet beat, but ♩. ♪ fits into two crotchet beats.

Grade 6

Specimen sight reading tests

Remember to use the ideas and techniques from the previous lessons when approaching sight reading.

Grade 7

Lesson 1

- **Practise reading** ♩₃♩♩

♩₃♩♩ fits into one crotchet beat.

Each triplet quaver lasts for one third of a crotchet beat.

Check the key signature. Look at the time signature, note values and other details, such as extensions and shifts. Then play the whole exercise.

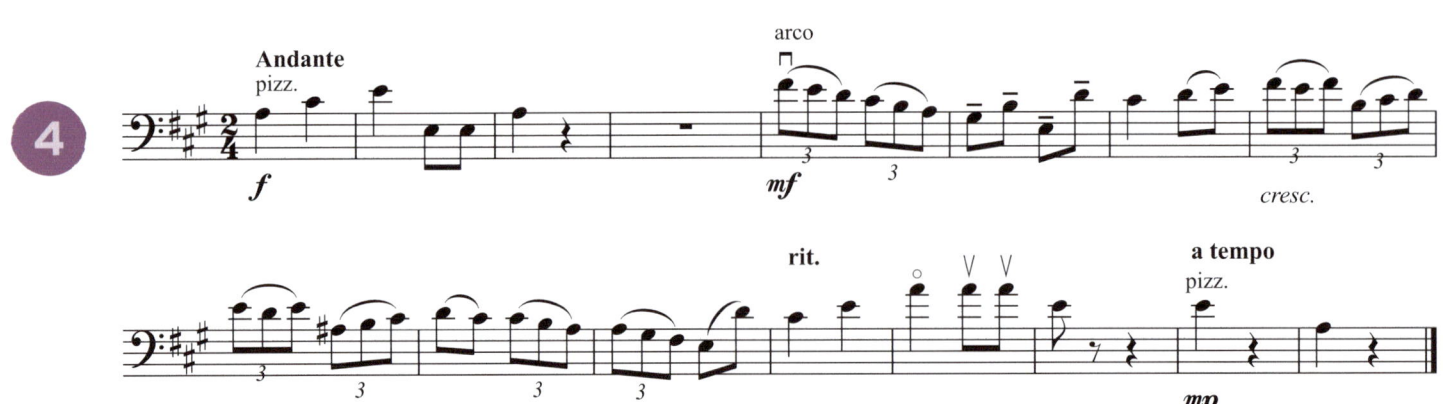

Grade 7

Speed read your part before you play. Check the following:

Key signature ☐   Extensions and shifts ☐

Time signature ☐   Double stops ☐

Scale patterns ☐   Retakes ☐

Accidentals ☐

 Set the pulse. Look at the tempo marking and the time signature, and subdivide the beat to work out a good tempo. Then silently count a full bar before you lead in.

Adapted from Haydn: *String Quartet* Op. 76 No. 3 (iv)

Remember that three triplet quavers fit into one crotchet beat. Keep a steady crotchet pulse ticking in your head as you play, and remember to keep counting on the longer notes too.

Grade 7

Lesson 2

- Practise reading in the compound time signature 9/8

  Nine quavers, or three dotted crotchet beats in a bar:

Check the key signature. Look at the time signature, note values and other details, such as extensions and shifts. Then play the whole exercise.

28

Grade 7

Speed read your part before you play. Check the following:

- Key signature ☐
- Time signature ☐
- Scale patterns ☐
- Accidentals ☐
- Extensions and shifts ☐

- Up bow starts ☐
- Articulation ☐
- Dynamics ☐
- Change to pizzicato ☐

 **Duet** Look at the tempo marking and the time signature, and listen carefully as your teacher sets the pulse in the first bar.

Adapted from Mahler: *Lieder eines fahrenden Gesellen* (iii)

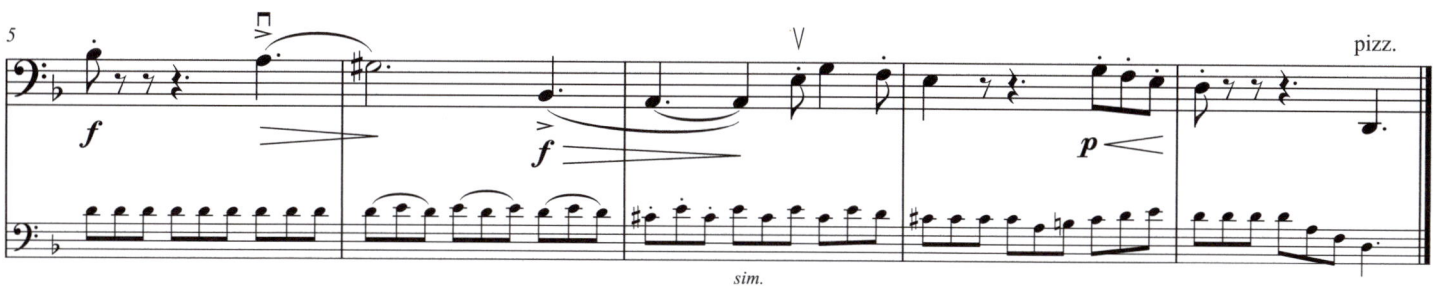

 Subdividing the beat is the best way to play rhythms accurately. Keep counting in the rests too.

Grade 7

Lesson 3

- **Practise reading in C♯ minor**

E major and C♯ minor share the same key signature:

Knowing your enharmonic equivalents is really useful and can make some notes that look unfamiliar feel more manageable, eg:

is enharmonically equivalent to:

Check the key signature. Look at the time signature, note values and other details, such as extensions and shifts. Then play the whole exercise.

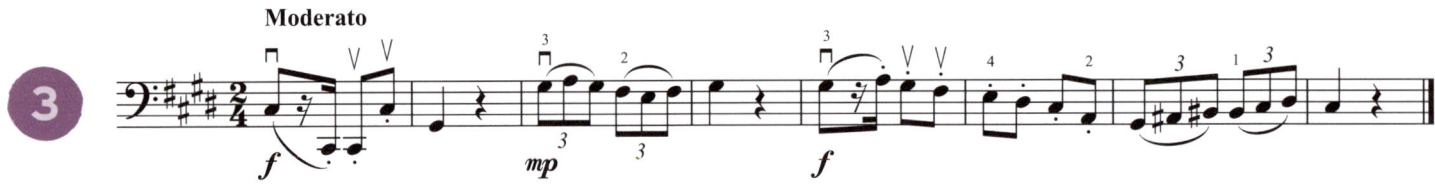

Grade 7

Speed read your part before you play. Check the following:

Key signature ☐   Extensions and shifts ☐

Time signature ☐   Extra up bows ☐

Scale and arpeggio patterns ☐   Dynamics ☐

Accidentals ☐

Set the pulse. Look at the tempo marking and the time signature, and subdivide the beat to work out a good tempo. Then silently count a full bar before you lead in.

Adapted from Beethoven: *String Quartet* Op. 131 (i)

In C♯ minor, the sharps in the key signature mean that the only open string you are allowed to play is the A string. Be careful though: A is the sixth degree of the scale, so it is often sharpened.

Grade 7

Lesson 4

- **Practise reading in F minor**

A♭ major and F minor share the same key signature:

As in A♭ major, when you play in F minor you will often need to use extensions and shifts because of the key signature.

Check the key signature. Look at the time signature, note values and other details, such as extensions and shifts. Then play the whole exercise.

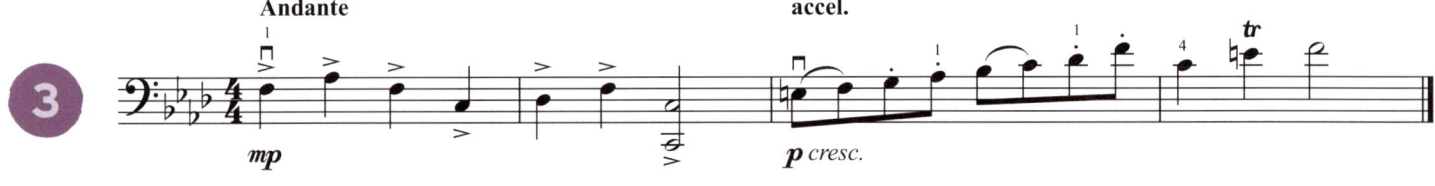

Grade 7

Speed read your part before you play. Check the following:

Key signature   ☐   Scale and arpeggio patterns   ☐

Time signature   ☐   Accidentals   ☐

Syncopation and notes tied over the bar line   ☐   Extensions and shifts   ☐

 Set the pulse. Look at the tempo marking and the time signature, and subdivide the beat to work out a good tempo. Then silently count a full bar before you lead in.

Adapted from Haydn: *String Quartet* Op. 20 no.5 (iv)

Count tied notes carefully - keeping a steady pulse ticking in your head will really help with this.

Grade 7

Lesson 5

- Practise reading in the key of B major

B major scale:

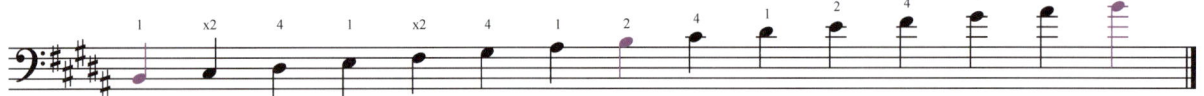

Remember that you will often need to use extensions and shifts because of the key signature.

Check the key signature. Look at the time signature, note values and other details, such as extensions and shifts. Then play the whole exercise.

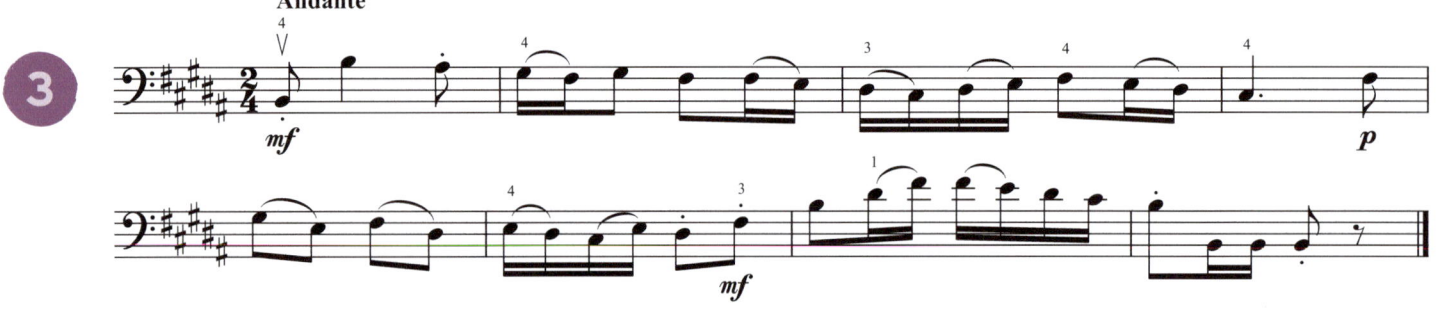

Grade 7

Speed read your part before you play. Check the following:

- Key signature ☐
- Time signature ☐
- Arpeggio patterns ☐
- Accidentals ☐
- Extensions and shifts ☐
- Dynamics ☐
- Articulation ☐

 Duet Set the pulse. Look at the tempo marking and the time signature, and subdivide the beat to work out a good tempo. Then silently count a full bar before you lead in.

Adapted from Haydn: *Symphony No. 46* (i)

 In B major, the sharps in the key signature mean that you are not allowed to play any open string unless there is a natural sign to cancel C♯, G♯, D♯, or A♯.

Grade 7

Lesson 6

- **Practise reading in D♭ major**

D♭ major scale:

Remember that you will often need to use extensions and shifts because of the key signature.

Check the key signature. Look at the time signature, note values and other details, such as extensions and shifts. Then play the whole exercise.

1

2

3

4

36

Grade 7

Speed read your part before you play. Check the following:

- Key signature
- Time signature
- Syncopation, and syncopated bowing patterns
- Scale patterns
- Accidentals
- Accents

Duet — Set the pulse. Look at the tempo marking and the time signature, and subdivide the beat to work out a good tempo. Then count a full bar out loud before you lead in.

Adapted from Tchaikovsky: *Piano Concerto* Op.23 (i)

When speed reading to plan your shifts, aim to avoid moving within a slur if possible.

Grade 7

Lesson 7

• **Practise reading shifts to 5th position (sharp keys)**

In sharp keys, the finger patterns in 5th position on the A string will usually start on F♯. The sharps in the key signature will show you the pattern of tones and semitones.

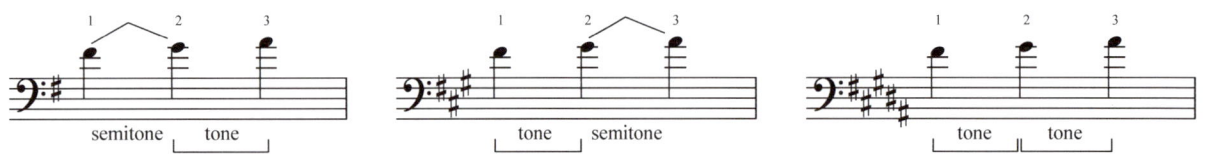

Check the key signature. Look at the time signature, note values and other details, such as extensions and shifts. Then play the whole exercise.

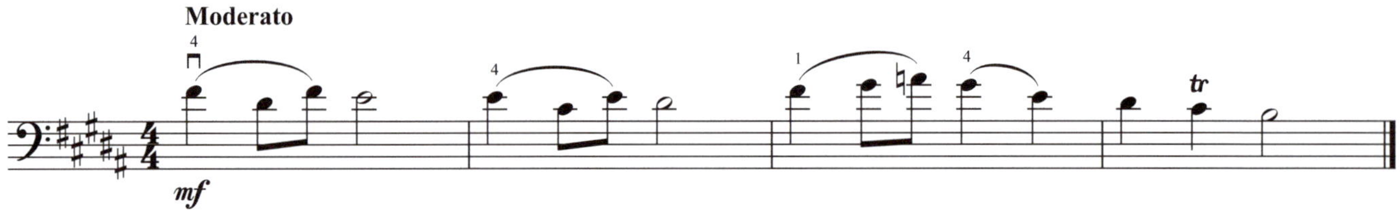

Grade 7

Speed read your part before you play. Check the following:

Key signature ☐   Extensions and shifts ☐

Time signature ☐   Accidentals ☐

Retakes and double up bow ☐   Accents ☐

 Set the pulse. Look at the tempo marking and the time signature, and subdivide the beat to work out a good tempo. Then silently count a full bar before you lead in.

Adapted from Mendelssohn: *Symphony No. 4* (i)

 String players can feel and see the difference between a tone and a semitone in their left hand fingers, as well as hearing it. Quick recognition of tones and semitones is important for good sight reading – know before you play.

Lesson 8

- **Practise reading shifts to 5th position (flat keys)**

In flat keys, the finger patterns in 5th position on the A string will usually start on F. The flats in the key signature will show you the pattern of tones and semitones.

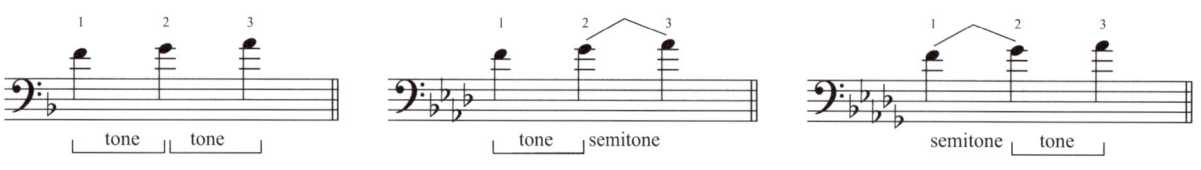

Check the key signature. Look at the time signature, note values and other details, such as extensions and shifts. Then play the whole exercise.

Grade 7

Speed read your part before you play. Check the following:

Key signature ☐   Accidentals ☐

Time signature ☐   Accents ☐

Extensions and shifts ☐

Set the pulse. Look at the tempo marking and the time signature, and subdivide the beat to work out a good tempo. Then count a full bar out loud before you lead in.

Adapted from Tchaikovsky: *Serenade for Strings No. 8* Op.48 (iv)

Even though you are 'only' sight reading, you should still aim to play as musically as you can.

Grade 7

Lesson 9

- Practise reading treble clef
- Practise shifting in and out of thumb position (A and D strings)

The notes you need to play in thumb position will usually be written in treble clef.

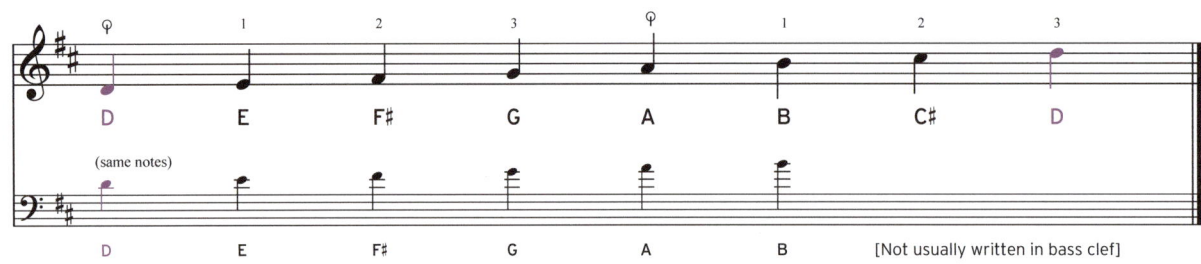

Check the key signature. Look at the time signature, note values and other details, such as extensions, shifts and clef changes. Then play the whole exercise.

Grade 7

Speed read your part before you play. Check the following:

Key signature ☐ Accidentals ☐

Time signature ☐ Accents ☐

Clef changes ☐ Dynamics ☐

Duet — Set the pulse. Look at the tempo marking and the time signature, and subdivide the beat to work out a good tempo. Then silently count a full bar before you lead in.

Adapted from Beethoven: *Violin Concerto in D* Op. 61 (i)

Practise playing in thumb position – play a scale of D major, then work out simple tunes such as *Frère Jacques* to help yourself become really familiar with the notes.

Lesson 10

- Practise playing music starting on an upbeat
- Revise the meaning of 𝄐
- Revise the meaning of *con sordino*

Sometimes the music that you play will start on an upbeat, or anacrusis. A one-note upbeat usually starts on an up bow. A two-note upbeat usually starts on a down bow. This is not always marked by the composer.

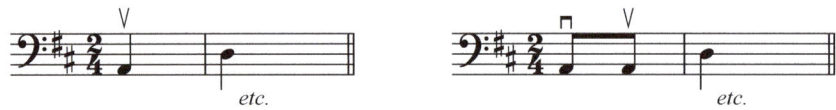

𝄐 means *fermata* 'pause'. Make the note or rest a little longer than usual.

con sordino is an instruction to tell the player to play with a mute. Make sure that you have a mute for Grade 7 sight reading tests and above.

Check the key signature. Look at the time signature, note values and other details, such as extensions, shifts and clef changes. Then play the whole exercise.

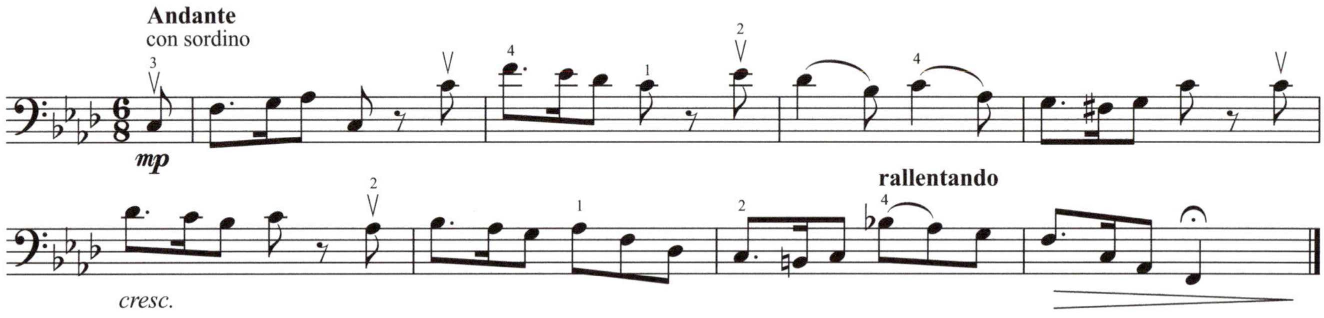

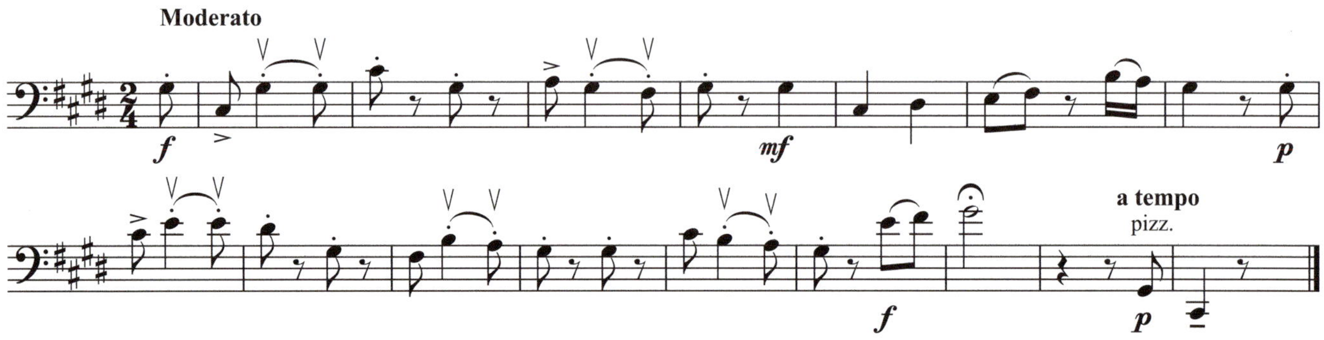

Grade 7

Speed read your part before you play. Check the following:

Key signature ☐   Accidentals ☐

Time signature ☐   Extensions and shifts ☐

Anacrusis ☐   Accents ☐

Clef changes ☐   Dynamics ☐

Duet — Set the pulse. Look at the tempo marking and the time signature, and subdivide the beat to work out a good tempo. Then silently count the correct number of beats before you lead in.

Adapted from Schubert: *Octet* D.803 (v)

Allegretto
con sordino

Knowing equivalent notes in different clefs is really useful. Remember that you won't necessarily need to play in thumb position in treble clef.

45

Grade 7

Specimen sight reading tests

Remember to use the ideas and techniques from the previous lessons when approaching sight reading.

[Blank page to facilitate page turns]

Grade 8

Lesson 1

- **Practise reading tenor clef**

The tenor clef is a 'C' clef — it shows where Middle C sits on the stave:

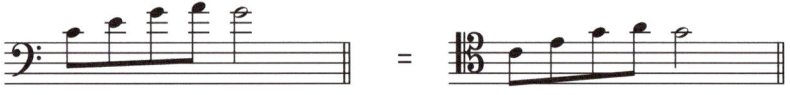

Sometimes higher notes are written in tenor clef in order to avoid too many ledger lines, eg:

Check the key signature. Look at the time signature, note values and other details, such as extensions, shifts and clef changes. Then play the whole exercise.

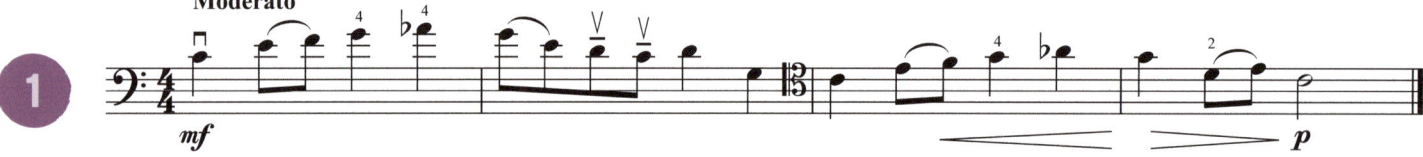

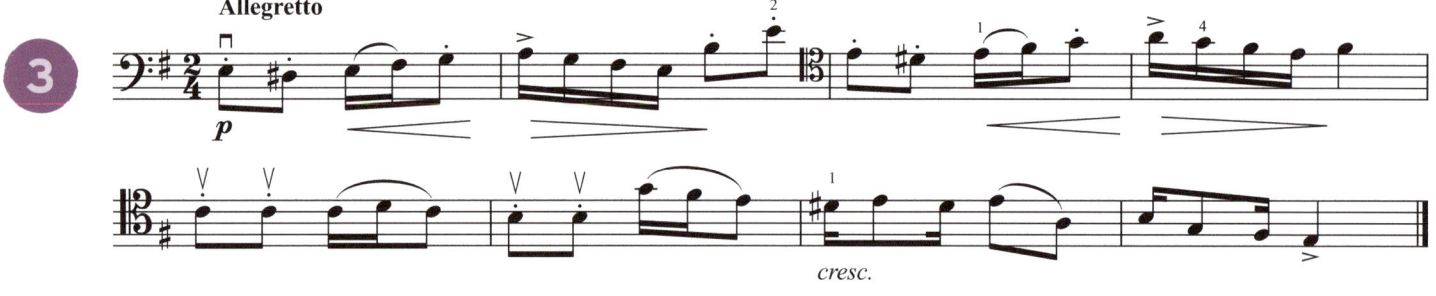

Grade 8

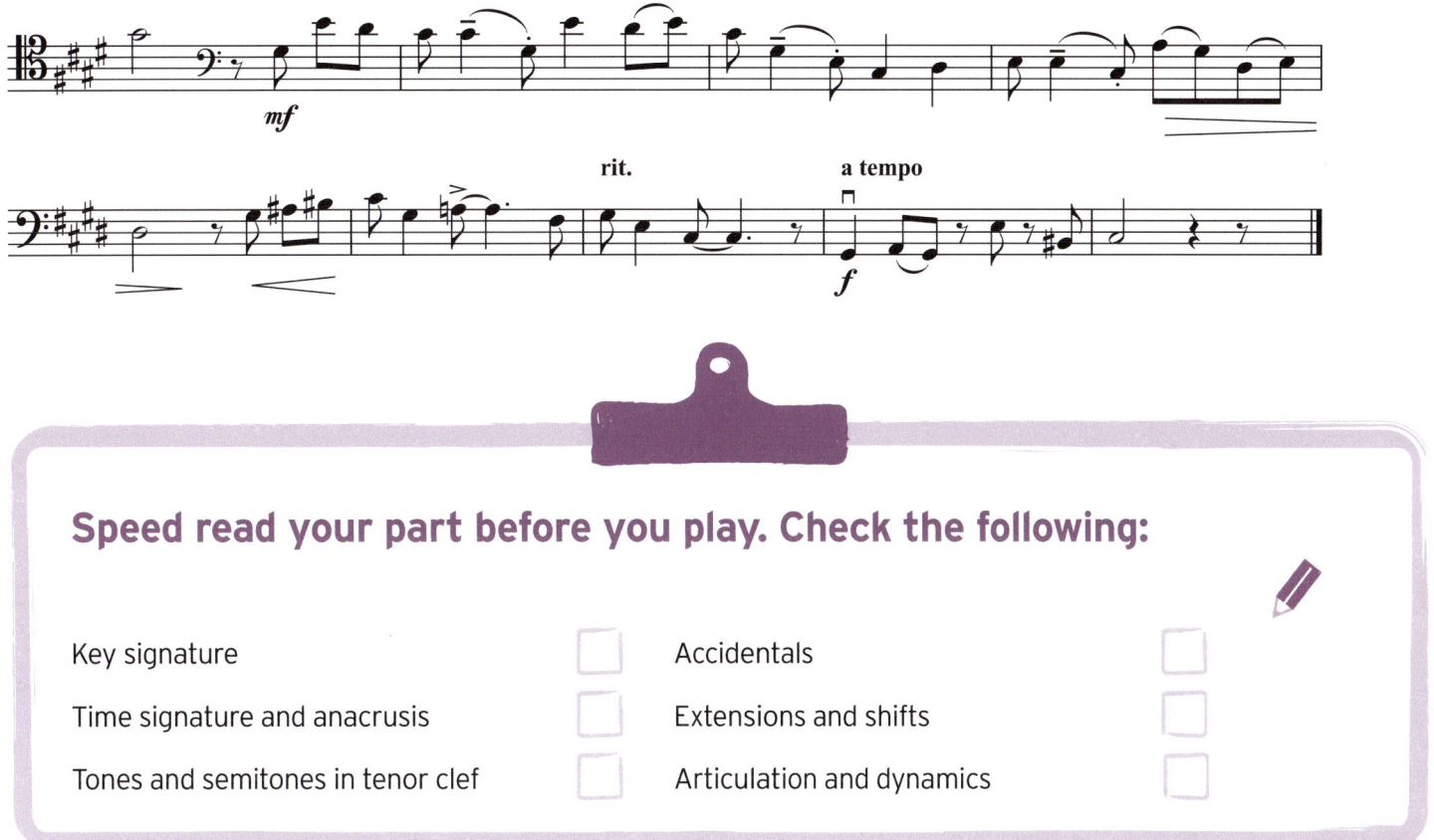

Speed read your part before you play. Check the following:

- Key signature ☐
- Accidentals ☐
- Time signature and anacrusis ☐
- Extensions and shifts ☐
- Tones and semitones in tenor clef ☐
- Articulation and dynamics ☐

 Set the pulse. Look at the tempo marking and the time signature, and subdivide the beat to work out a good tempo. Then silently count two quaver beats before you lead in.

Adapted from Dvořák: *Symphony No. 4* (iii)

 When speed reading through, remember to plan your shifts. Try to avoid moving within a slur if possible.

Grade 8

Lesson 2

- **Practise reading duplets**

Duplets tell you to play two notes in the time of three.

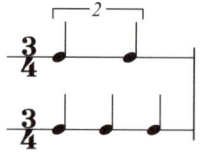 A pair of duplet crotchets lasts for three crotchets.

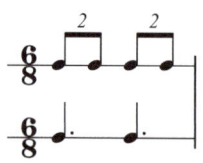 A pair of duplet quavers lasts for three quavers (or one dotted crotchet).

Check the key signature. Look at the time signature, note values and other details, such as extensions, shifts and clef changes. Then play the whole exercise.

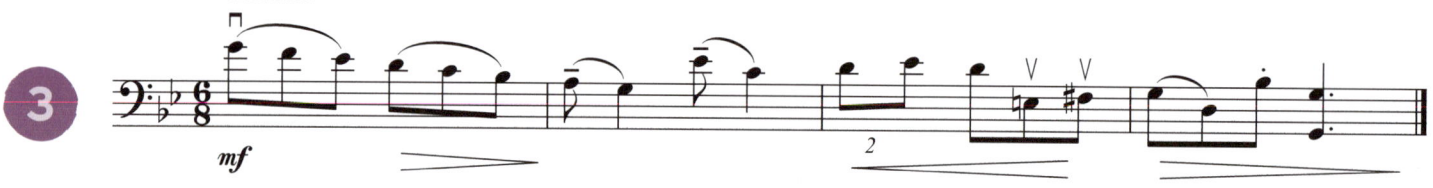

Grade 8

Speed read your part before you play. Check the following:

Key signature	☐	Shifts	☐
Time signature	☐	Chords	☐
Duplets and extra up bows	☐	Articulation	☐

Set the pulse. Look at the tempo marking and the time signature, and subdivide the beat to work out a good tempo. Then count a full bar out loud before your teacher begins.

Adapted from Brahms: *Symphony No. 4* (iii)

In compound time, counting in dotted crotchet beats rather than quavers will make it easier to play duplets.

55

Grade 8

Lesson 3

- **Practise reading irregular time signatures**

At this grade, you may be expected to sight read the following new time signatures:

$\frac{5}{4}$ (five crotchets in a bar) $\frac{5}{8}$ (five quavers in a bar) $\frac{7}{8}$ (seven quavers in a bar)

These time signatures are called *irregular* time signatures because the beats cannot be divided equally within the bar. Practise playing your scales in fives and sevens to become familiar with the feel of these time signatures and the different possible groupings of notes, eg:

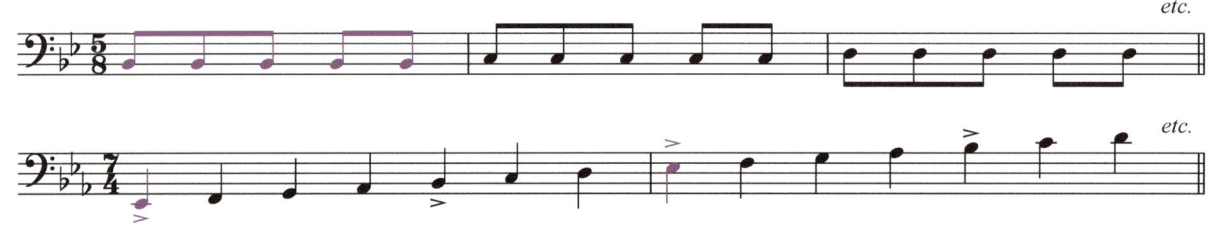

Check the key signature. Look at the time signature, note values and other details, such as extensions, shifts and clef changes. Then play the whole exercise.

1

2

3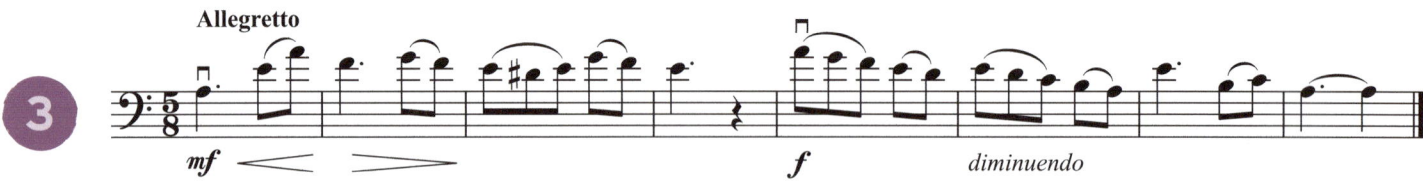

4

Grade 8

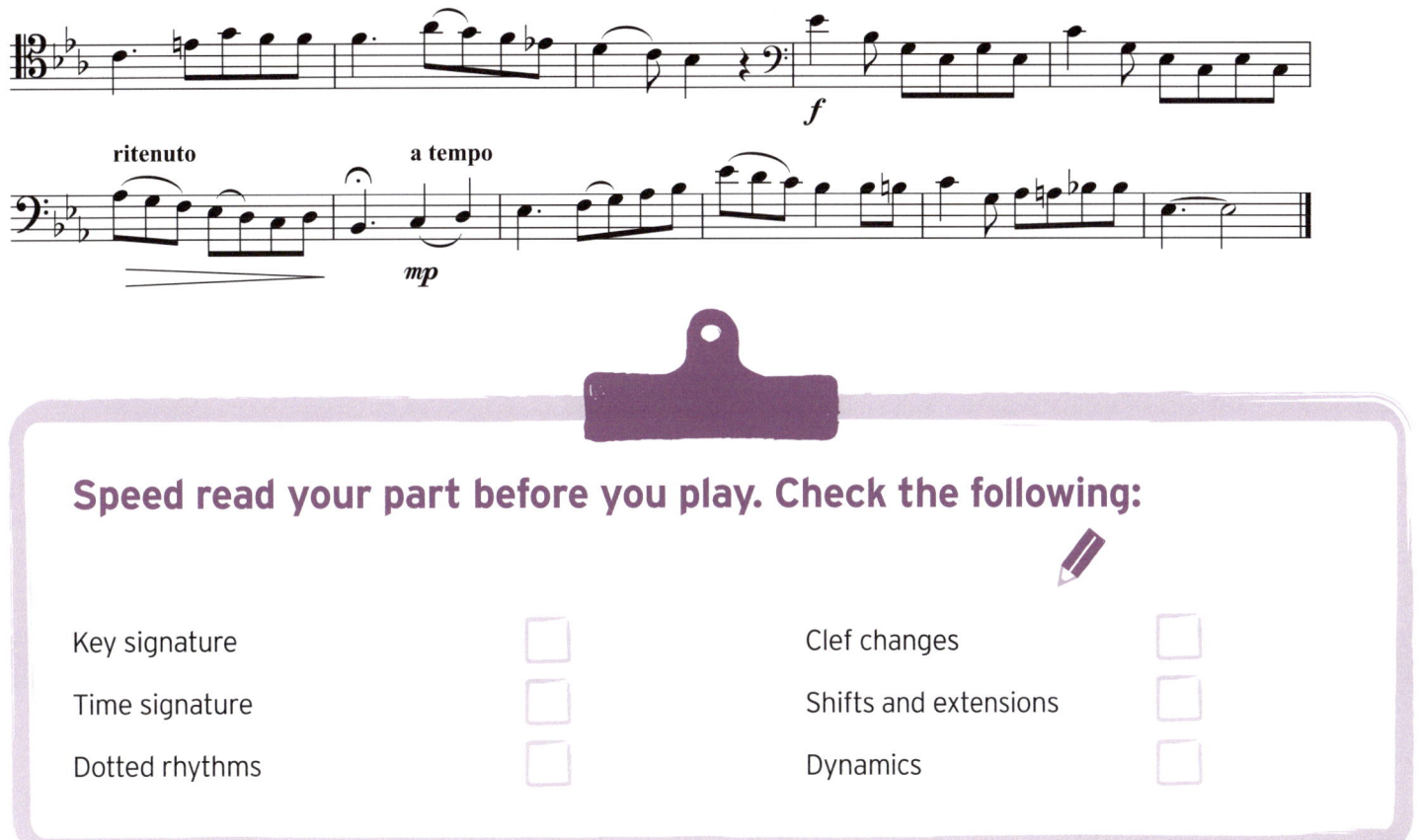

Speed read your part before you play. Check the following:

- Key signature
- Time signature
- Dotted rhythms
- Clef changes
- Shifts and extensions
- Dynamics

Set the pulse. Look at the tempo marking and the time signature, and subdivide the beat to work out a good tempo. Then silently count a full bar before you lead in.

Adapted from Tchaikovsky: *Symphony No. 6* (ii)

Although it is tempting to stay in 1st position as much as possible, it is often more sensible to use other positions in order to avoid awkward string crossings.

Lesson 4

- **Practise reading changing time signatures**

Time signatures may change during a piece of music. Unless indicated, the pulse stays the same, so keep counting and carry on.

When the time signature switches between compound or irregular time and simple time it always helps to subdivide the beat to ensure that the quaver pulse remains consistent.

Check the key signature. Look at the time signature, note values and other details, such as extensions, shifts and clef changes. Then play the whole exercise.

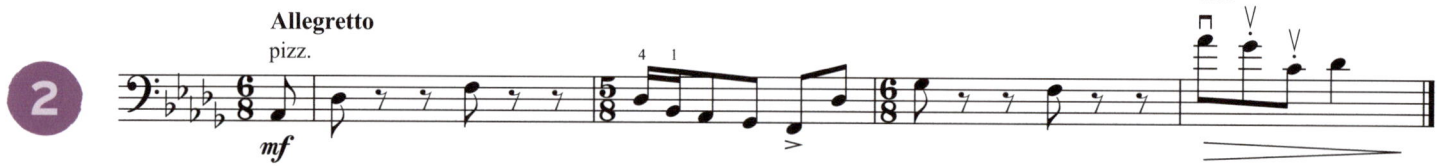

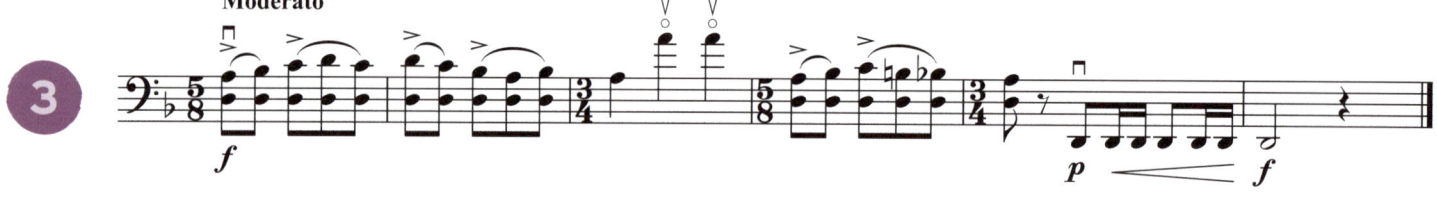

Grade 8

Speed read your part before you play. Check the following:

Key signature ☐   Shifts and extensions ☐

Time signature (and changes) ☐   Accidentals ☐

Clef changes ☐   Dynamics ☐

Dotted rhythms ☐

 **Duet** Set the pulse. Look at the tempo marking and the opening time signature, and subdivide the beat to work out a good tempo. Then silently count a full bar before you lead in.

Adapted from Brahms: *Lieder und Gesänge* Op.59 No.5

Time signature changes at the end of a system are useful to help you to prepare for the next bar. Always try to read ahead so that you are as prepared as possible for what is coming up.

Grade 8

Lesson 5

- **Practise reading double stops**

At this grade double stopping may include two stopped notes (ie no open string), eg:

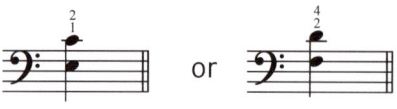

Check the key signature. Look at the time signature, note values and other details, such as extensions, shifts and clef changes. Then play the whole exercise.

Grade 8

Speed read your part before you play. Check the following:

- Key signature ☐
- Time signature ☐
- Double stops ☐
- Dotted notes ☐
- Accidentals ☐

Look at the tempo marking and the time signature, and listen carefully as your teacher sets the pulse in the first bar.

Adapted from Vivaldi: *Gloria*

Wherever possible, read ahead and prepare your hand for the next double stop.

Lesson 6

- **Practise reading treble clef**

Here is a reminder of the treble clef notes you need to know and play in thumb position.

D E F# G A B C# D

See page 42 if you need to remind yourself where these notes are in bass clef.

As you learnt in Grade 7, treble clef doesn't necessarily mean that you need to play in thumb position.

Check the key signature. Look at the time signature, note values and other details, such as extensions, shifts and clef changes. Then play the whole exercise.

Grade 8

Speed read your part before you play. Check the following:

Key signature   Changes from arco to pizz.

Time signature   Harmonics

Clef changes   Shifts to thumb position

 Set the pulse. Look at the tempo marking and the time signature, and subdivide the beat to work out a good tempo. Then silently count a full bar before you lead in.

Adapted from Mahler: *Symphony No.1* (i)

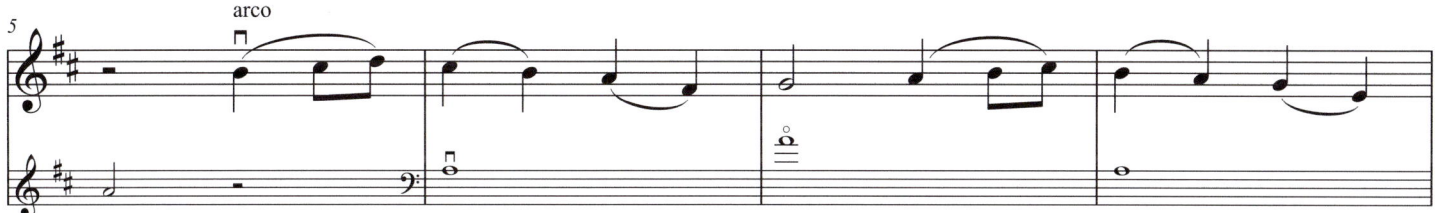

There is often a choice about when to shift. With thumb position it often pays to prepare early, eg. in this duet you could start in thumb position in bar 1.

Grade 8

Lesson 7

- **Practise reading in 2/2 or ¢**

2/2 or ¢ Two minim beats in each bar.

Music written in 2/2 time looks similar to music written in 4/4 time, but quavers tend to be beamed in fours and there is a feeling of two main beats in each bar.

Check the key signature. Look at the time signature, note values and other details, such as extensions, shifts and clef changes. Then play the whole exercise.

Grade 8

Speed read your part before you play. Check the following:

- Key signature ☐
- Time signature ☐
- Clef changes ☐
- Shifts and extensions ☐
- Accidentals ☐
- Dynamics and articulation ☐

 Set the pulse. Look at the tempo marking and the time signature, and subdivide the beat to work out a good tempo. Then silently count the correct number of beats before you lead in.

Adapted from Schubert: *Symphony No. 5* (i)

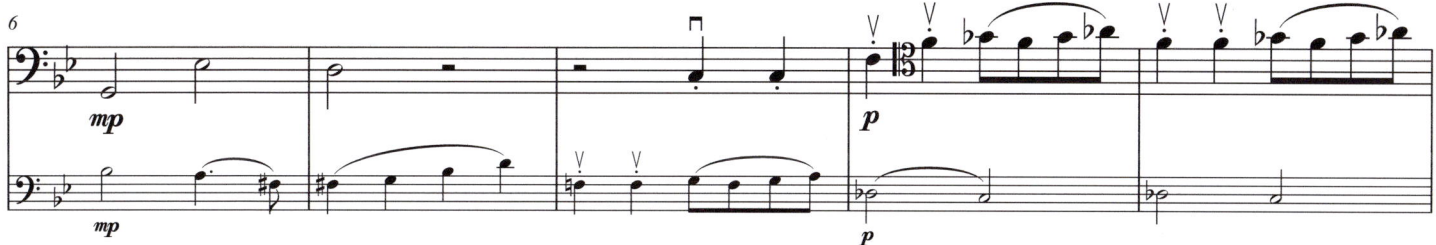

Try to train your eye to focus in on potentially tricky moments (eg. the G flats in the duet above). This will mean that you can make the most of every second of your preparation time.

Grade 8

Lesson 8

- **Practise reading in G♯ minor**

B major and G♯ minor share the same key signature:

Watch out for double sharps (𝄪). F𝄪 is enharmonically equivalent to G.

Check the key signature. Look at the time signature, note values and other details, such as extensions, shifts and clef changes. Then play the whole exercise.

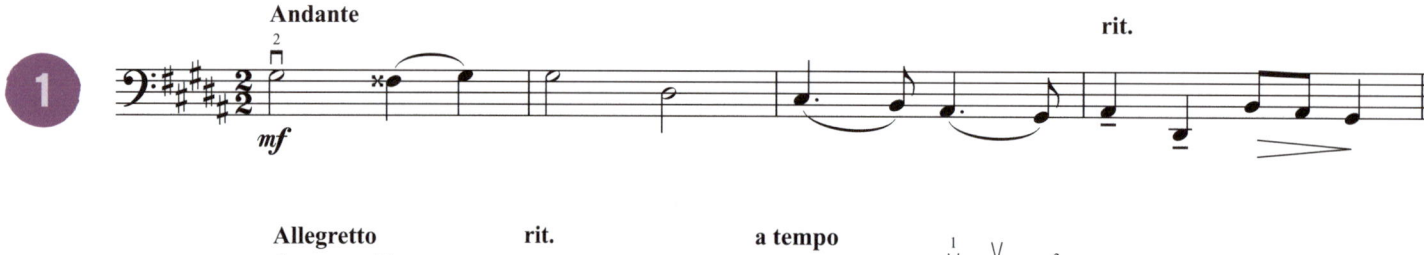

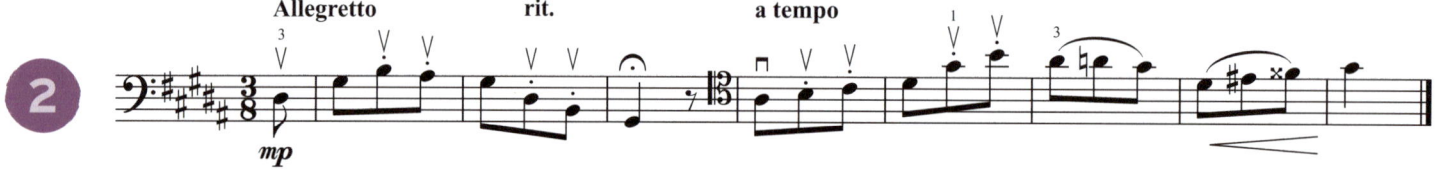

Grade 8

Speed read your part before you play. Check the following:

Key signature ☐   Shifts and extensions ☐

Time signature ☐   Accidentals ☐

Anacrusis ☐

 **Duet**

Set the pulse. Look at the tempo marking and the time signature, and subdivide the beat to work out a good tempo. Then silently count two dotted crotchet beats before you lead in.

Adapted from Mussorgsky: *Pictures at an Exhibition*

When playing music with lots of sharps or flats in the key signature, think very carefully indeed before you play an open string.

67

Lesson 9

- **Practise reading in B♭ minor**

D♭ major and B♭ minor share the same key signature:

As in D♭ major, when you play in B♭ minor you will often need to use extensions and shifts because of the key signature. Remember that all open string notes apart from C are usually flattened in these keys.

Check the key signature. Look at the time signature, note values and other details, such as extensions, shifts and clef changes. Then play the whole exercise.

Grade 8

Speed read your part before you play. Check the following:

Key signature ☐   Shifts and extensions ☐

Time signature ☐   Accidentals ☐

Triplet semiquavers ☐   Dynamics ☐

Changes from arco to pizz. ☐

 **Duet**

Set the pulse. Look at the tempo marking and the time signature, and subdivide the beat to work out a good tempo. Then count a full bar out loud before your teacher begins.

Adapted from Tchaikovsky: *Marche Slave*

Remember, when setting the pulse, always think about how fast you are happy to play the shortest note values in the piece.

Grade 8

Lesson 10

- Practise reading more Italian terms and techniques

Glissando: 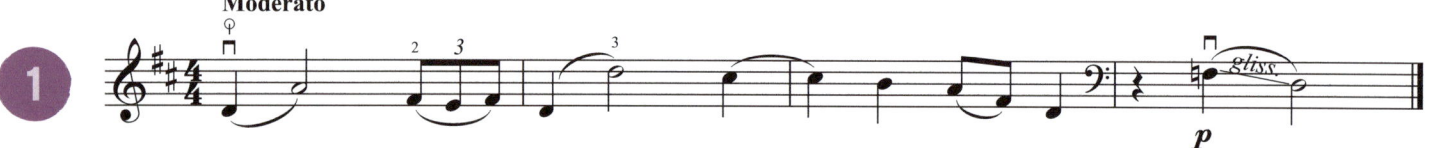 Slide your finger from one note to the next.

Left-hand pizzicato:  Pluck the strings with your left hand.

Natural harmonics:  Touch the string where shown, and play the note as a harmonic.

Check the key signature. Look at the time signature, note values and other details, such as extensions, shifts and clef changes. Then play the whole exercise.

Grade 8

Speed read your part before you play. Check the following:

Key signature(s) ☐   Changes from arco to pizz. ☐

Time signature ☐   Harmonics ☐

Triplet semiquavers ☐   Left-hand pizz. ☐

 **Duet**   Set the pulse. Look at the tempo marking and the time signature, and subdivide the beat to work out a good tempo. Then silently count a full bar before you lead in.

Adapted from Haydn: *Symphony 45 ('Farewell')* (iv)

 You may occasionally encounter a key signature with more than five sharps or flats. Keep calm, count up the sharps or flats, and remember that you will usually need to avoid open strings.

Grade 8

Specimen sight reading tests

Remember to use the ideas and techniques from the previous lessons when approaching sight reading.

Grade 8

10

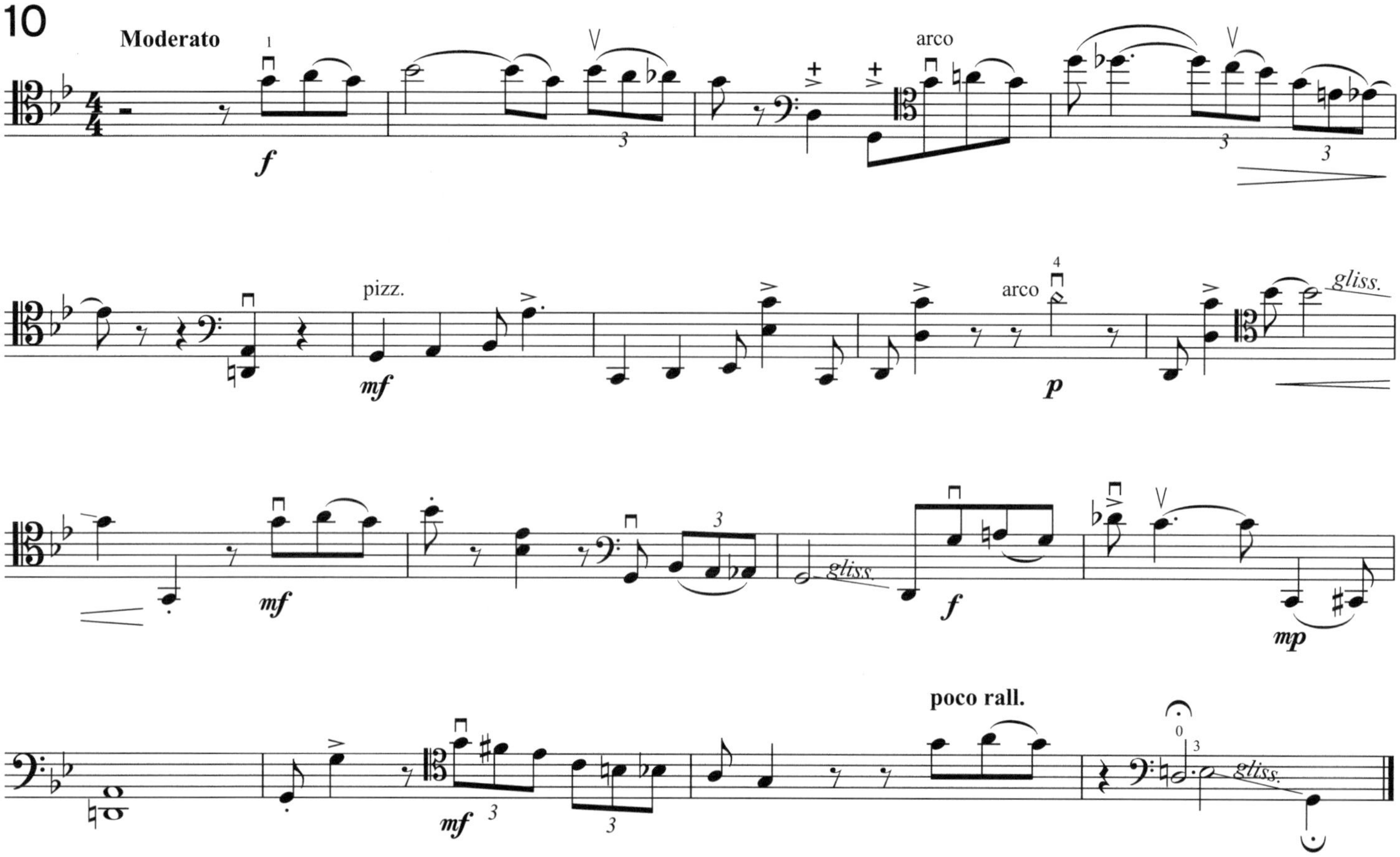
Moderato
arco
pizz.
arco
gliss.
gliss.
poco rall.
gliss.

11

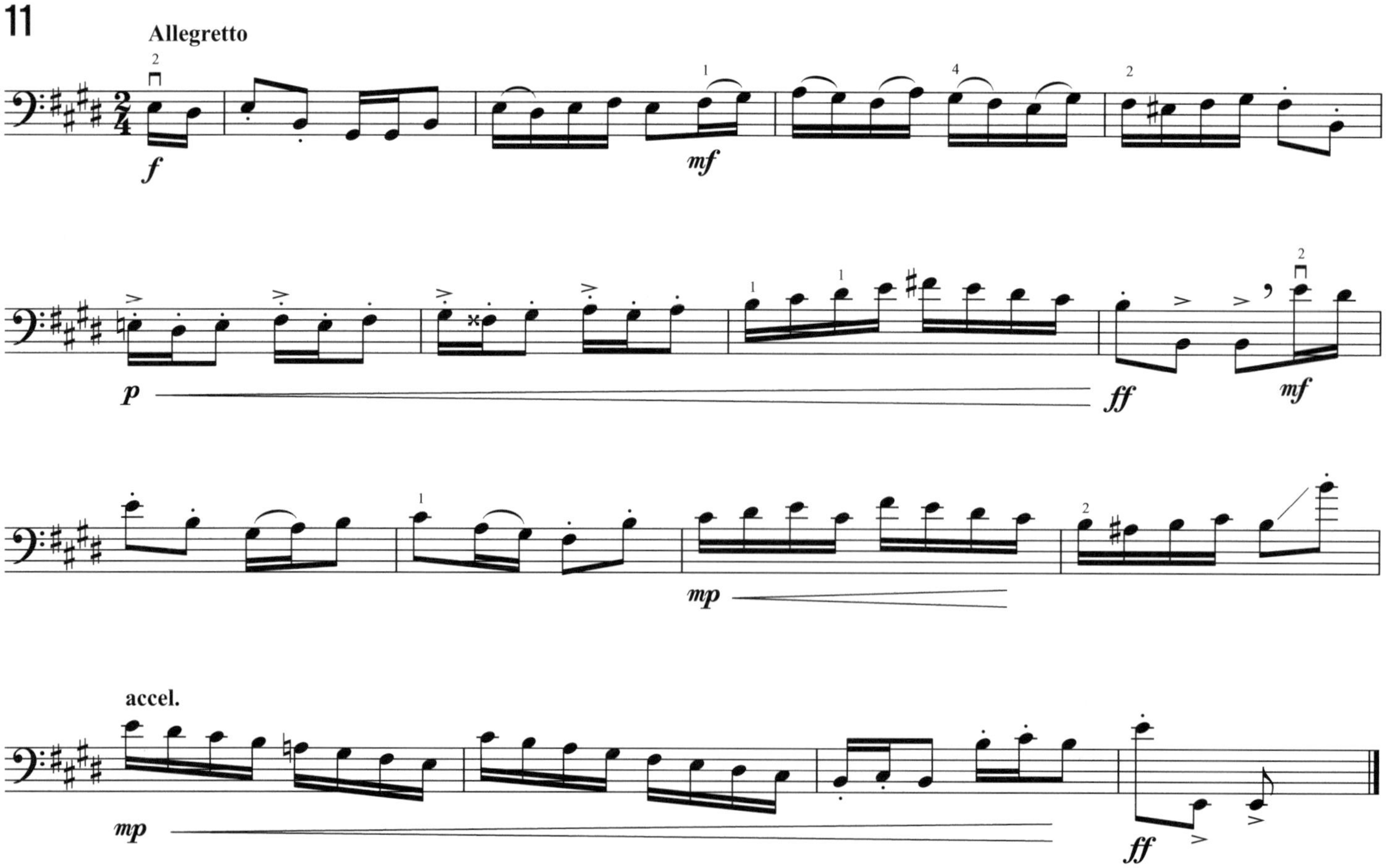
Allegretto
accel.